# Once There was a
# Caterpillar

For Meriel - J.A

For Hannah, Carl, Heather
and little miss trouble! - M.G

First published in 2009 by Wayland

Copyright © Wayland 2009
This paperback edition published in 2009 and 2011 by Wayland
Wayland, 338 Euston Road, London NW1 3BH

Wayland Australia
Level 17/207 Kent Street
Sydney NSW 2000

Editor: Nicola Edwards
Designer: Paul Cherrill
Digital Colour: Carl Gordon

British Library Cataloguing in Publication Data

The right of Judith Anderson to be identified as the
author of the work has been asserted by her in
accordance with the Copyright, Designs and Patents
Act 1988.

Anderson, Judith, 1965-
Once there was a caterpillar
1. Caterpillars - Juvenile literature 2.
Lepidoptera - Life cycles - Juvenile literature
I. Title II. Gordon, Mike
595.7'8139

ISBN: 978 0 7502 6682 6

Printed in China

Wayland is a division of Hachette Children's Books,
an Hachette UK company.
www.hachette.co.uk

# Nature's Miracles

# Once there was a
# Caterpillar

Written by
Judith Anderson

Illustrated by
Mike Gordon

WAYLAND

Caterpillars are amazing!
Some are hairy. Some have
spots or stripes.

And some of them live in my mum's cabbages.

A caterpillar starts as a tiny egg.

6

These eggs are stuck to this leaf. They can't fall off.

Look!

Caterpillars hatch out of their
eggs in the spring. They are
tiny. And very hungry.

8

They start to eat straight away.
Leaves are their favourite food.
In fact, leaves are their only food!

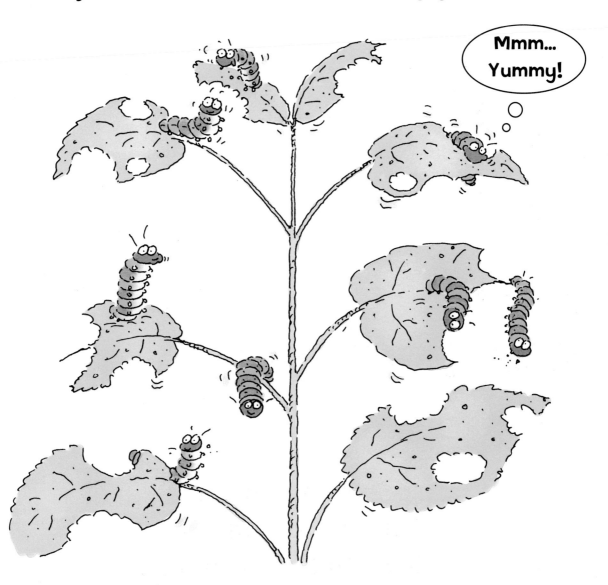

As they eat,
they grow.

They grow so quickly that they soon grow out of their skin.

Luckily, new skin has already grown underneath the old skin.

# This happens quite a few times!

By the end of summer,
the caterpillars have
grown big and fat.

But they don't stay caterpillars for ever. They change.

Time to go!

First they shed
their skin one last
time. Then they
attach themselves
to a nice leaf or twig.

Next they make a hard shell to protect themselves. This is called a chrysalis. The chrysalis looks just like another leaf or twig.

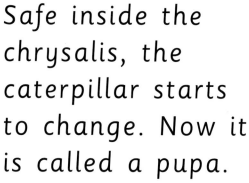

Safe inside the
chrysalis, the
caterpillar starts
to change. Now it
is called a pupa.

It loses its fat
body and starts
to grow long legs,
and wings.

This change is called metamorphosis.

Then, when the pupa is ready, it breaks out of the chrysalis.

Ah, that's better!

But it isn't a pupa anymore.
The pupa has become a
beautiful butterfly.

The butterfly warms
itself in the sun.
Then it flies off to
look for food.

Butterflies don't eat leaves. They drink sweet nectar from flowers.

That's not the end
of the story, though.

After the winter, the female
butterfly returns to the same
kind of plant or tree where
it first hatched out.

It lays some new eggs
on a leaf, and soon these
eggs hatch into a new
family of caterpillars.

So the caterpillar's story starts all over again. It is called a 'life cycle' because it goes round and round.

# NOTES FOR PARENTS AND TEACHERS

## Suggestions for reading the book with children

As you read this book with children, you may find it helpful to stop and discuss what is happening page by page. Children might like to talk about what the pictures show, and point out the changes taking place in the young caterpillar.

The idea of a life cycle is developed throughout the book, and reinforced on the final pages with the diagram of the eggs, caterpillar, chrysalis and butterfly. Ask the children if they know of any other life cycles. Can they see any patterns in nature? The other titles in the series may help them think about this.

Discussing the subject of caterpillars and butterflies may introduce children to a number of unfamiliar words, including chrysalis, pupa, hatch, nectar and metamorphosis. Make a list of new words and discuss what they mean.

## **Nature's Miracles** and the National Curriculum

The **Nature's Miracles** series satisfies a number of requirements of the Science curriculum at Key Stage 1. There are four titles about cycles in nature in the series: *Nature's Miracles:*
*Once There Was a Seed; Once There Was a Caterpillar;*
*Once There Was a Tadpole* and *Once There Was a Raindrop.*
Each book encourages children to explore the natural world for themselves through direct observation and specific activities and emphasises developing a sense of responsibility towards plants, animals and natural resources.

**Once There Was a Caterpillar** will help young readers to think about how caterpillars and butterflies are part of the world around them, in line with the unit on 'Plants and animals in the local environment'. The book also provides learning and discussion opportunities for units on 'Variation', 'Habitats' and 'Life cycles' by introducing children to the idea that caterpillars and butterflies require specific conditions and adaptations for survival.

## Suggestions for follow-up activities

The children in this book discover that some caterpillars and butterflies like cabbages best. If you want to attract a wide variety of caterpillars and butterflies into a garden or playground, talk to the children about how different species lay their eggs and feed on different plants, and try growing some of their favourites such as nasturtiums, lavender and honesty. Buddleia will also attract many species of butterfly.

Remember, too, that butterflies need shelter and warmth as well as food. If you are making a butterfly garden, choose a sunny spot, out of the wind, and check that there is a source of water from a puddle or shallow dish set into the soil. Some species also like rotting fruit such as apples or pears.

Alternatively, try looking for caterpillars and butterflies in wild areas, as several common species favour nettles, thistles or ragwort. Encourage the children to note down the insects they see and the plants on which they find them. Do, however, remind the children that nettles and thistles will sting and prickle if touched!

31

# Books to read

*The Very Hungry Caterpillar* by Eric Carle (Puffin, 2002)
*The Case of the Missing Caterpillar* by Sam Godwin and Simone Abel (Wayland, 1999)
*Looking at Lifecycles: Butterfly* by Victoria Huseby (Franklin Watts, 2007)

# Useful websites

www.kidzone.ws/animals/butterflypics/monarchpicstory.html
www.tooter4kids.com/LifeCycle/Butterfly_Life_Cycle.htm

# Index